AF265381

137

by

Carol Winteringham

Published by Threepeppers Publishing

1ˢᵗ Edition – April 2018

ISBN: 9780995727465

Cover:
Blue Front Door at 137 Victoria Road in 2015
Photo © Carol Winteringham

www.3peppers.co.uk

To Mum and Dad

Contents

Introduction

Even though I have spent most of my life living in various parts of Italy, I still consider myself English and make every effort to go back home as often as possible to soak up the English way of life. Living away from your home country does make you see it in a different light and it makes you think more about what you have left behind. When I started looking back I suddenly realised that all my years in Leeds, England, had been spent at one address only: 137 Victoria Road. All my childhood years and early experiences stemmed from here.

I have had a busy life teaching and bringing up two children so for a while my background got pushed aside to the back of my mind for more important duties. However, in the last few years I have become more nostalgic and simply had to go back to see where I used to live and where I spent so many happy years growing up. We, as a family, had been back to Headingley, a neighbourhood of Leeds, on several occasions after the death of my Dad in February 2000 but it was always a fleeting visit or just a drive past. On one of the latter occasions, when we were in Leeds to celebrate a Winteringham family reunion, both Janet and her family together with mine went strolling down familiar streets from Otley Road, past the Original Oak Pub and St Michael's Church where I got married, down Bainbrigge Road and Cardigan Road onto Victoria Road to take a good long look at our house. Naturally, it was filled with memories.

I enjoy writing, and although I have never actually written a book of any kind before, I felt I wanted to put down on paper some of those memories. My family probably will have heard a lot about these memories already but reading it on paper in a book is different because it means they will last forever. I have enjoyed writing it as a way to remember my Mum and Dad and all the happy years gone by. I hope it is a pleasant read for all.

This book has been published this year, in 2018, because I have reached a milestone in life. I will be celebrating my 70th birthday in April.

Chapter One
How it all started

I remember once upon a time, a long time ago, when I was training to become a Primary School teacher, we were given a Geography project as one of our assessments. Geography had always been one of my favourite subjects right from the day I got a large book for Christmas, all about the geography of the world. If my memory does not error, I must have been about six years old. Mind you this college project did not take me very far out into the world as it was about the percentage and type of facilities available in the residential area of Headingley, Leeds, where I was born and raised.

Headingley was, and still is, a large suburb on the northern edge of the inner city of Leeds. It had always had a certain elegance about it with its wide tree-lined roads and large detached houses as well as its terraced houses. These houses were originally built for the middle classes who could afford servants. Even back in the 1960s, however, it was beginning to lose that elegance as it had become very popular with students for accommodation as the large Victorian houses lent themselves excellently to being split up into student flats.

I started on my project and my first stop was the City Council Office to look at town planning maps so I could outline better the area under study. I got a shock when I found out that the road I lived on had been doomed for demolition as soon as possible but in any case before 1980. How could they even consider pulling down the beautiful terraced houses on Victoria Road! Such beautiful architecture, I thought, such robust houses. No one could believe it nor understand why they would want to pull down such beautiful houses. They had named it the "twilight zone", goodness knows why. Anyway, I started on my project, written and drawn by hand as there were no computers back then, and I thought this could become a really important piece of work for me as it could describe an area which might quickly disappear or be totally transformed into something unrecognisable. I wanted to remember Victoria Road as it had always been.

Well, we are now in the year 2018 and someone on the Town Council must have had a change of heart or maybe simply funds did not reach that far because the houses are still standing and the area is just as thriving as it was back then. Certainly, the houses along Victoria road were grand houses, sturdy and built for large well off Victorian families. They have certainly withstood the test of time.

On the odd occasion, when I can, I like to go back there with my extended family and reminisce. Our house was always affectionately referred to as 137. However, I remember that when I was living at 137 I was not always so proud of it, sometimes even thinking it was old fashioned and out of date as so many new modern houses with mod cons like showers and central heating were being built. I would not go so far as to say I was embarrassed by where I lived, but almost. Then again, having a large house had its advantages, such as when we had family, lodgers and friends to stay or when there was a birthday party or some other celebration. There was always plenty of room for everyone.

One day, around 2009, while working on my computer I received an interesting e-mail from my sister Janet who had been doing some on-line house hunting for some reason and had quite by chance come up with a house for sale on Victoria Road for £350,000. It was our house 137! She had immediately sent me pictures of the exterior and even some of the rooms inside. I was overwhelmed to be able to look back inside the house I had lived in ever since I was born, for over 24 years. I became quite nostalgic and it was this that sparked off the idea to put a few words down on paper for my now grown up children and grandchildren. A few words that would give them an idea of what life was like at home at 137 with my Mum and Dad, little sister Janet and our lovely dog Gyp in the years between 1948 and 1970.

Image 1 - Front of 137 Victoria Road in 2015

Image 2 - Back of 137 Victoria Road in 2015

Chapter Two
What a lot of rooms

Whatever can this be? A word which has almost disappeared from use these days. It was our working kitchen which was a long narrow area attached to the living room on the ground floor and separated by a step down and a door.

Our scullery was my Mum's working kitchen where she did most of the cooking and washing. It was very plain and basic but it did the job. It had a gas cooker and a modern cabinet on one side. We kept all the basic food stuffs in the cabinet which had a modern pull-down leaf to work on and compartments to store things like bread or sugar and tea. On the other side there was a large window. It looked out onto the back yard which was a paved area and below the window was a large ceramic sink. These sinks have come back into fashion again and are considered quite trendy but they only remind me of how many plates and glasses got cracked if they just slightly touched the side of the sink. Not at all practical!

There were other cupboards too and later on a washing machine appeared but that was much later on as I remember my Mum washing all our clothes and bedding by hand in the large sink. She also had a wrangler, which was a strange device where you pushed clean, wet clothes through so

15

as to drain off excess water. It involved a lot of hard work. The still wet clothes were then hung outdoors to dry.

There was linoleum on the floor which was changed every so often to give the room a fresh look. My Mum never had a dishwasher or a fridge, never mind a freezer or tumbler dryer. She always washed clothes by hand and Monday traditionally was washing day, just like in the old nursery rhyme. Hanging clothes out to dry on zig-zag washing lines in the garden was a job in itself. As a child, I loved playing with my sister running and hiding between the sweet-smelling sheets and clothes.

Our fridge was a special room. It was a long dark narrow room under the stone steps at the front of the house. The large stone slabs kept the room stone cold as they say and so it was the perfect fridge. It was freezing inside there even in Summer. My Mum could put a Rowntree's strawberry jelly or freshly made trifle in there on a Sunday morning and it would set quickly in time for Sunday tea. Yet again this was not one of my favourite rooms, and neither my sister nor myself enjoyed going inside there as it was dark and on occasions there were spiders too. It had two really long shelves where we kept all the food cold especially, at Christmas time when we had turkey or pork pies. Later on, when frozen food began to come onto the market and we bought things like Bird's Eye frozen fish fingers, they too were kept for as long as possible in this cold room which we called the pantry, which is another word which seems to have disappeared from use.

The scullery had a coal cellar at the opposite end. This was a very cold dark room made black by all the coal deliveries over the years. It was a frightening room and the place Dad would send Janet and myself and make us stay there for what seemed like hours when we misbehaved. For instance, if we didn't wash our necks! It was a place to be feared. Apart from the sheer darkness, mainly because there were no lights there, it was full of spiders, something I detested as a child. When I or my sister were sent there, we knew we had done something wrong, but I don't think we deserved such a terrible punishment.

The coal cellar had a square hole on one side with a door which could be opened when the coal men came in winter to deliver bags of the stuff. Coal was the main fuel for heating at 137 and large quantities of it were needed in the winter months. I would love to share with you a really funny incident which has been told and re-told over the years and still sticks in my memory as such a hilarious escapade. On the eve of my wedding day which was to be held on 7th September 1974, we had had a good night out drinking with friends and family as it was custom, and then we all returned back to 137 for a night cap. Everyone was in high spirits. My brother in

Image 3 – The Kitchen in 2015

Image 4 - The Coal cellar in 2015

law, Chris, had a good time chasing one of my best friends, Norma, a good-looking girl, around the house. She foolishly decided to hide in the coal cellar to get away from him. Chris is extremely tall, with really long legs. He opened the little door leading into to the cellar and climbed in to catch her which was no easy job as the hole was tiny. They both appeared a few minutes later, black, covered in coal dust with Norma feeling very disgruntled about the whole matter.

It was still common at the time to find outside toilets, something which we no longer see today. This was part of the long scullery building but access was only from the outside. It was just a toilet and we often used it even in winter rather than having to climb three flights of stairs to the bathroom on the second floor, but it was a cold, dark room with no lighting.

Our Living Room or Kitchen

This really was the heart of the house as it was the place where we spent most of our time as a family. The room was fully wall-papered and carpeted from wall to wall. It also had a really interesting feature which we kept for many years and never completely parted with. Opposite the large fireplace, high up on the far wall, almost at ceiling level, there was a long wooden panel which had about five bells hanging from it. Each bell was placed at the same distance one from another and they were connected to the Front Door and the various upstairs rooms, mainly the bedrooms. 137 was built as a fine Victorian house for a relatively well-off middle class family who probably had one or more servants. This area of the house was originally the working area for the servants and the owners upstairs would ring, or should I say pull, one of the bells when they needed some more coal or other services. As children, my sister Janet and I were really taken in by this system which still worked well and we could ring the bell from one of the rooms upstairs by pushing or pulling a very elegant knob. What a system they had invented. Later, we got rid of the bells, which was a shame, but they dated the house considerably. The only one which stayed with us forever was the elegant Front Door bell that had to be pulled hard to make it work.

The first fireplace I remember in the living room was very old fashioned. It must have been Victorian. It was enormous and took up most of the wall. It was made of black iron and had a large fireplace with a stove for cooking on and a small oven with a door. It was used a lot and you could even toast bread for example using a toasting fork. Behind it there was the water tank, and the fire heated the water for us. We had a fire every day, all day in winter, and it must have been hard work to have to keep the fire going all day without ever letting it go out. I remember how Janet and I used to try and get warm by the fire after we had been outside for hours playing in the snow, making snowmen, and how we tried to dry off our wet gloves and boots.

I also remember vaguely a very chaotic few days. I must have been about four years old, when the water heater behind the fireplace burst. It was quite a common thing in those days and it caused havoc. We got up one morning to find the kitchen flooded. I remember the water going everywhere. Mum and Dad had the dreary task of lifting up furniture and carpets and putting them outside to dry. We lived upstairs for a while until it was sorted. Many years later, a new modern fireplace was installed with a new gas system. They had recently discovered large supplies of gas in the North Sea and all houses were to get this new supply. The days of coal were over. The new fireplace came with this gas supply and we got to choose the style and colour we wanted. In the end we picked a light-coloured marble effect, quite bright after the black iron. It also had a very pretty mantelpiece to put things on like a clock or ornaments. It was a shame to see the old fireplace go but it was for the better. Progress, they say. However, I came to really dislike the new fireplace because I cut my forehead badly twice on one of the sharp edges of the mantelpiece. Maybe I was rocking on a rocking chair. I can't remember how it happened but I remember suffering two nasty cuts and having a thick plaster on them for days.

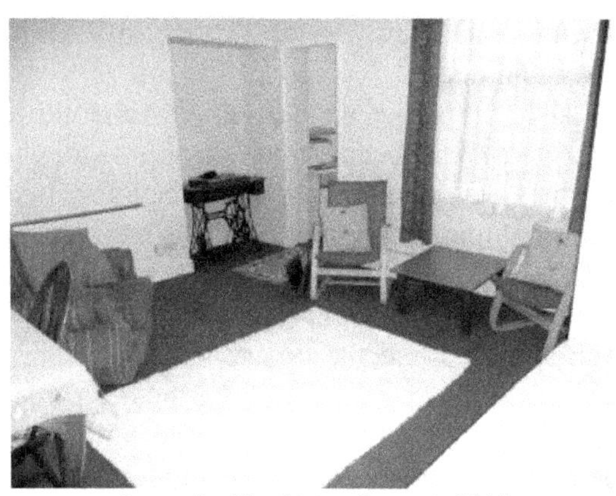

Image 5 - The Living Room in 2015

*Image 6 - The TV and Carol's 21st Birthday Cake in the
Living room (1969)*

There was a large round table in the middle of the room which could easily sit eight people. It was made of good quality wood but it was a heavy piece of furniture so it was never moved around. It was nice though and I spent many Sunday mornings dusting and cleaning it together with other heavy pieces of furniture. The large table in the centre of the room took up a lot of space but we made great use of it. We always had our meals there and Mum used it when she was doing a lot of cake baking and needed space as the scullery was very narrow to work in. We would spend hours making cakes, buns, scones, Christmas cakes, with all the ingredients spread out over the table. It was also where Dad would do his Friday accounts and I would help him put coins into piles of sixpences, shillings, half crowns and so on. I always did my school homework on this table when I was younger but it was also the table where we played so many board games during the Christmas holidays. Games like Snakes and Ladders, Ludo, which I used to love, and popular card games. This was also the "entertainment" room but more about that later in the book.

A large window opened onto the back yard and garden and we could see who was arriving at any moment. Under the window there was the writing desk which was beautiful. A leaf opened down so you could write there. It had lots of small compartments for letters, envelopes, ink and so on. Next to the fireplace there were two large armchairs. One was for Dad and trouble brewed if Janet or myself thought we could sit there when he was around. It was his chair. As I got older, I used to annoy Dad by taking his place. I seemed to get some kind of pleasure from pinching his seat, and still don't know why to this day! The other armchair was for my Mum. She sat on the right of the fireplace, my Dad on the left. Later though, there was a settee for two or three people so we could all sit next to the fire. Maybe I annoyed Dad by taking his chair because I thought we should all have the opportunity to sit close to the fire.

When I was about four I think, Mum and Dad bought their first television set, which was a special event in our household like in every other house in the 1950s. In one corner of the kitchen there was a fine oval table in dark wood. My parents kept the large wireless there. By 'wireless', I mean today's radio. We often spent Sunday afternoons and evenings listening to the songs on the wireless, such as "Sing something Simple", and Janet and I would often put on shows for Mum and Dad singing and dancing to these songs. There was also a children's hour with songs and stories just for children which I adored. Of course, when the large television set came along, everything had to be moved around and the wireless was pushed into another corner to make way for this enormous piece of modern equipment. Television programmes did not start until five o'clock with "Children's Hour". There was just one channel to watch and no commercials. We were so taken with this new device that we would turn it on before the programmes started just staring at the test screen waiting patiently and eagerly.

There was also a Singer sewing machine in the kitchen when I was small. My Mum used to love sewing and making lovely party dresses. She would spend a lot of her free time being very creative. I particularly remember a pink net party dress. Janet had one exactly the same and we wore them to go to cousins Pauline and Christine's birthday party at their home in Horsforth, another area of Leeds. It was so pretty. I am only sorry I don't have a photograph of me wearing it but I remember the dress well even so. Mum was a very able dressmaker and made lots of our clothes as well as sewing costumes and tutus for our ballet concerts. She stayed up until late making penguin outfits, policeman costumes, crinolines and raffia skirts just to name a few. You name it, Mum made it!

At one end of the square room, under the array of bells, there was Janet's piano. Janet practiced her lessons here and when she had learnt some new pieces we would all sit and listen. When she learnt some more popular songs or Christmas Carols we even sang along. We often had family singing sessions on a Sunday afternoon.

We had a back door leading into the back yard and small garden, and stairs leading up to the fine blue Front Door and main entrance onto Victoria Road itself. Close friends, deliveries or workmen came to the back door while visitors or guests came to the Front Door. The door leading off the kitchen took us to the steep flight of stairs to the first floor as well as the Front door. It also led to the large under stairs pantry used as a fridge, and on the left, there was the sitting room. Just behind the kitchen door was a large space where we kept our coats, bikes and other stuff. I suppose it was a sort of cloakroom. There was a long, dark wood, heavy sideboard in the corridor. It was full of interesting drawers of all shapes and sizes where kept all sorts of things, from gloves and scarves to cello tape, glue and pens. It was a truly Victorian piece of furniture, so old-fashioned but well made. It was often a problematic piece of furniture because it was so big and bulky it was difficult to find a space where it would fit. It was also far too heavy to move about. After being put in this suitable corridor it was never moved again.

When the bell rang in the kitchen it meant there was someone at the Front Door and our fit dog Gyp would virtually leap up the stairs four at a time, to be the first to answer the door. He would push past you in order to be there before you. Then it was probably only my school friend Norma who had come for a chat but Gyp would not stop barking until someone had opened the door. I remember these stairs well too because I fell down them on two occasions and cut my forehead badly. There was a lot of blood but in those days they just put a thick plaster on it and that was the end of it. I still have the scar to remind me of when they ripped the plaster off and I screamed from the pain.

The Sitting Room

This room was almost in a semi basement with a large bay window which overlooked a small garden and higher up we could just see people passing on the pavement on the main road, Victoria Road. It was a bit dark. It was also a cold room. However, there was a nice fireplace and so a fire was often made which kept the room nice and warm for special occasions. We did not use this room every day. It was a special occasions room. Birthday parties were held here and Christmas Parties too. I also had my twenty-first birthday party here. There was no television set here but I played my new record player and transistor here when I was a bit older. We also used this room to play table tennis. My best friend Norma would come and pay a visit and join in. It was also here where I tried to beat my cousin John from Birmingham. You can imagine it was obviously quite a large room and a place where we had a lot of fun. It had a lovely carpet, curtains and a three-piece suite placed around the fireplace. Later on, when I was bit older, this room became the dining room for our University student lodgers during term time. We rarely used the room then.

Next floor up: the First Floor

There were two large rooms leading off the landing on the first floor, which was actually the ground floor if you came in through the Front Door on Victoria Road!

One room was my parents' bedroom which was huge and overlooked the back of the house onto the Norwoods. The other was a bedroom for our lodger Joe, who I remember very little about. The room looked out onto Victoria Road itself. Later it became my sister's bedroom, then a study room and finally a guest room. My Italian brother-in-law Carmelo and his new wife, Anna, slept in this room when they came to England for their honeymoon in 1975. Both rooms on the first floor were large with high ceilings and stucco around the walls. They both had large fireplaces too. The one my sister used often had a fire on in it. It was a very nice, bright room and you could see a good part of Victoria Road from the large bay window.

Janet and I would spend many Sunday mornings playing in my Mum's bed, dressing up, making tents and playing games. It was often four in a bed and we used to sing "Roll over, roll over and one fell out" over and over until usually someone did fall out. The room had a very nice suite of furniture: there was a large double wardrobe with a long mirror inside where Janet and I would look at ourselves when we played at dressing up. There was a 'tallboy', a kind of chest of drawers where Mum kept all her bed linen. There was an oval table in one alcove next to the fireplace which was never used. The room had two very large windows and the bed was opposite them. What fun we had in this room!

Back on the landing, we had an unusual coat stand which could literally hold hundreds of coats. It was an enormous piece of furniture but useful at the same time. It had a mirror, drawers and umbrella stands, one on each side as well as lots of hooks for coats. You can imagine how much it was used when we had five students staying with us as well as ourselves. I don't think any modern house today would have sufficient space for such a huge piece of furniture. The landing was well carpeted wall to wall and up the long flight of stairs to the next floor. It was big event when we changed the carpet here and there were discussions as to the colour and design we should choose. The last one I remember was dark green with black flecks in it, which in my opinion was very elegant and suited the house well.

The staircase was really beautiful as it had a beautifully carved banister in a light-coloured wood leading up to the second floor. I really liked this banister and I often used to polish it with a nice lavender furniture polish. As you will have gathered, dusting the furniture was my "Sunday job" but I must admit I did not hate doing it.

The Second Floor

There is so much to say about this floor that it is difficult to know where to start from so I might as well start from the beginning. Firstly, my Mum used to live in this house before she got married but she didn't occupy all of the house. My Mum Dorothy, or Dot as Dad would call her, was born in Birmingham and moved to Leeds when she got a job as a stenographer or secretary for a large firm in Burley called Marsdens. I have never known the exact date when she moved into 137. I only know that when Mum and Dad got married this was the house they lived in but they did not use all of the house because this floor was occupied by their close friends Jim Brown and his wife Betty who had just got married. They must have stayed there for a few years although I do not have any memory of them so maybe they had moved out by the time I was three or four. They moved to another part of Headingley but always remained close friends with the family. Jim Brown was one of Dad's closest friends when they were young and later he always went to the Oak pub to see Dad and play bowls. I always remember him smoking a pipe.

When I was a bit older, I had a room of my own which was the first room on the left when you reached the top of the stairs. It looked out over the back of the house, over the Norwoods. It had a small fitted wardrobe which I really liked and a fireplace which was occasionally lit in the early days. I would enjoy choosing colour schemes for the walls and fitted carpet. It did not have a lot of furniture: just a bed, a dressing table with three mirrors, plus a table and chair where I used to try and study when it was near exam time. One of the things I enjoyed doing was changing the furniture around every so often to give the room a fresh look. I did not have a radio or stereo or suchlike in the room unlike nowadays. I used to put posters on the walls of my room and put keepsakes and souvenirs on the mantelpiece.

The room was always mine even when I moved away for three years to go to college in Ilkley. When I used to come home during holidays then my room would be waiting for me.

The other rooms on this floor remained empty and unused for a while but at a certain point, probably when Janet and I took up most of Mum's time and she was no longer able to go out to work, my parents decided to take in student lodgers which would become Mum's source of income. The bedroom opposite mine was very similar in that it also had a fitted wardrobe and a fireplace but it had two large windows that looked out over

Victoria Road, which was a pleasant view but over time, as traffic increased, it became quite a noisy road so it was no longer a quiet room.

The Kitchenette

Next to the above-mentioned bedroom there was what we called the kitchenette. It was a kitchen to all effects: it was a long, narrow room with a large window at the end. It had a sink in one corner. The kitchenette and the empty bedroom became students' bedrooms. Two students occupied the larger room and one rented the kitchenette which became a very cosy room. This is the room where Mimmo, my boyfriend at the time, stayed when he came to England for the first time to meet my family. Next to the kitchenette, there was a tiny store room where students kept their suitcases and other stuff but we never used it. Next to the store room and my room there was the bathroom.

The Bathroom

This was Victorian furnishings at its best! It was definitely original and I wonder if it still exists, or have they pulled it out because it has become so out-dated. We thought it was outdated when we were living there and it was bit embarrassing when we knew that newer houses were installing modern bathroom suites and showers. We never had a shower because we had an enormous bath. Really enormous! It was almost the length of the

Image 7 - Carol's bedroom in 2015

Image 8 - The Bedroom on 2nd floor in 2015

bathroom wall and so deep. It took a lot of water to fill it but there was nothing nicer than soaking in it with water up to the brim. The taps were very elegant with both a hot and cold tap. It was quite difficult to get in and out of too. You had to climb in! It must have been quite a modern feature in its day, as it was one long piece of furniture made entirely of wood. Quite unusual now if you think bathroom suites today are made of ceramic. The bath continued onto the sink area with a surround where we could put toiletries and things. There was a nice mirror over the sink and a dividing wooden panel separating the toilet from the rest. The toilet area was enormous too with a large surround all made of wood which today probably wouldn't be considered hygienic. The inside of the toilet had an elegant light blue willow pattern of plants and flowers. It really was unique. Everyone who has been to 137 or lived in it has made comments on this toilet and some friends even remember it to this day. That is how unique it was! The room had a bath-chair to rest your clothes on while you were having a bath. This is the chair I brought to Italy as a keepsake when Dad decided to move to another house, which is now looking well in our bedroom. The bathroom had linoleum on the floor and two small bath rugs. It had no heating so when you got out of the bath in Winter it was pretty cold which meant you dried yourself very quickly and made your way downstairs to get dry in front of the fire and also dry your hair as there were no hair dryers either when I was very little. Dad used to rub our hair dry with a towel. He was quite heavy handed about it and we used to complain out loud! When there were students staying from October to June we all had to share this bathroom so the outside toilet was convenient at times.

Next floor up: the Attics and the Box Room

There were two large attic bed rooms, one on each side of the house with the tiny box room separating them in the middle. The scary thing was going up the last flight of stairs at night and seeing the large skylight above you. It was a large window in the roof made of large glass panels which revealed the dark open sky above us. However, as we got older, both Janet and I liked the idea of sleeping up in the attics. Like all attics they had low sloping ceilings and a square skylight. One of them even had the large square water tank which provided all the water for 137. Mum and I decorated the attics. We usually had one room pink and the other one light blue with flowered wallpaper. Janet and I didn't mind sleeping there but it could get a bit scary in the Winter months when the bad weather came along, bringing strong, gale force winds which often blew off the chimney pots. We could hear them rolling down the roof and it sounded as if they would come crashing in at any minute. Then, when it snowed heavily during the night, the noise of snow sliding down the roof would wake us up. I think the howling winds were the worst though.

However, even though Janet and I slept in the attic for many years, I always considered the room on the floor below as my room, even today! Janet also shifted between the large front room on the first floor and the attic. It was quite a novelty being able to choose bedrooms.

The box room was called as such precisely because it was a tiny square room rather like a box chock-a-block, full of all our old junk accumulated over the years, from plastic inflatable characters and dolls houses, to old school books and Christmas decorations and lots more. It had no light in it so we could only go there to sort or find things during the daytime.

Well that's it! That was the layout of the interior of my house: ten rooms altogether!

Image 9 - The Blue Front Door at 137

Chapter Three
Our Lodgers

I believe it was Mum's idea to make the best use of so much space when she could no longer fit office working hours into her timetable, having two young children to look after. Surely the extra income would have been useful.

I wonder though if she realised how much hard work it would involve. We had five or six students living with us at a time, all males. We even had some foreign students staying with us at times. I remember one from Iceland with a strange surname, Thorenson Thorenson I believe! I remember Chris Swan who studied Early English Literature and a boy with ginger hair who came from Bakewell (like the tart of the same name). He studied Geography and got me interested in the subject. There was also a strange little man, whose name I forget, but he studied statistics and he really was an odd number! A large number of students enjoyed Mum's cooking and the way she looked after them. Many of them stayed for all three years, others came and went but there were so many I can't remember them all. Mum provided breakfast and evening meal - so she cooked for ten people every day. She would make them a cooked breakfast if they wanted it, at 8 a.m. The evening meal was always two courses plus cheese and biscuits, so she was kept very busy. She also used to tidy their rooms and change their beds, and even wash and iron bed linen and towels. Remember there was no washing machine back then – I don't know how she managed it! At weekends students had all their three meals: breakfast, lunch and dinner unless they went home to see family, but most of them stayed in Leeds during term time. So Mum constantly cooked for ten people every day from October to June each year, and then thankfully, there was the Summer break. When I was a teenager I used to help Mum prepare things for them and I used to take food in and out of the dining-sitting room. I also used to help with all the washing up, done by hand every evening. However, the students were never a problem. They were very quiet, they were out most of the day but even when they were at 137 they never made a lot of noise, not even when they came back in the early hours of the morning during the weekend.

As if this wasn't enough work, Mum also took in guests during the Summer. One group I remember well was the Jehovah's witnesses. They were becoming a strong religious group at the time and became very popular. They had large meetings in Leeds over the Summer which lasted three to four days and they were constantly looking for lodgings. So Mum occasionally provided them with rooms and meals.

When these rooms were empty during the Summer months, Janet and I, and all our friends, used to play all over the house. We made up some very imaginative games –like treasure hunts and the "ghost room", a kind of maze in the dark. We used blankets and clothes horses, anything we could lay our hands on to create strange labyrinths we had to go around alone in the dark. How bizarre! But what fun we had! I remember my friends: Norma, Sholto, David and Ian Falgate from across the road, Janet's best friend Linda Markham, Janet's boyfriend Robert Jackson, Susan Nutter and many more.

Chapter Four
The Garden

137 had a small garden at the back. The part nearer to the back door was paved but it had a small flower bed outside the scullery window where Mum kept the odd plant. Mum would hang her washing in this part of the outer area or on warm Summer days we would get the chairs out to sunbathe. Janet and I often used Mum's washing line to make a swing by tying the ends of the line on each side of the garden area. What fun we had. Most of our family photos outside were taken here near the back door.

 Further down there were some flower beds which Mum carefully looked after, planting her lovely little blue and white flowers as borders. Snap dragons, alyssums and carnations, these were some of her favourites. There was a small square of lawn where we would sit or lie in Summer on warm days and have picnics or even put up a tent to play and have lunch inside. Around the edges of the lawn were flowers. On one side was a lovely rose bush which bloomed faithfully and lasted all the time we lived at 137. Near the dustbins there was a large patch of rhubarb, a common feature in Yorkshire gardens. Mum used it a lot to make rhubarb pie or crumble with custard. There was once a laburnum tree on the street side with its lovely yellow-orange flowers but when someone said it was poisonous it was cut down. Our garden was only small but we liked it and used it a lot. We even lit a bonfire here on 5th November for bonfire night and invited the Markhams and others for some parkin (a gingerbread cake popular in Yorkshire) and hot drinks.

The back garden basically stayed the same for all the years we lived there, no major changes were ever made, maybe because we liked it as it was.

The front of the house did not have a garden but a small sloping area which was difficult to manage, and in fact we never really knew what to put there. Sometimes Mum planted flowers, then a bush, then grass but sometimes nothing at all. The sitting room bay window looked out onto this area so we tried to make an effort to make it look nice but it was difficult.

Chapter Five
Objects I still care about

This may come as a strange title for a chapter in a book but I can well assure you it is a true statement. Even after so many years there are some pieces of furniture or other household objects that remain vividly in my mind and when I start looking back, going down memory lane, these same old objects come hauntingly back to me as if we had never parted and they had never disappeared. It is true when people say we become attached to certain familiar objects and grow fond of them without really knowing why.

One strange piece of furniture which also has a kind of story attached to it is my Mum's Singer sewing machine. My Mum was a wizard dress maker cum costume maker. Janet, my sister and I went to dancing lessons for many years and the school also put on shows periodically which we always took part in, as a solo or as a dance team. Janet's famous piece was the policeman ("If you want to know the time, ask a policeman!"), and mine was a sailor's hornpipe dance. And let's not forget 'Happy feet' when we dressed up as penguins! Mum made all our dance costumes with patient loving care that only a Mum has. She bought all the materials, braids, sequins and much more, made the patterns, cut them out and started sewing. Sometimes she would stay up until very late to finish something off. The sewing machine was her companion. It had various places in the house over the years – in the kitchen, in a bed room, in her bedroom. This latter place was where I caught a left toe, the third one, on the pedal of the sewing machine and my toe nail came off. It was very painful. I also remember vividly catching my finger nail under the needle on the machine when I was learning to sew and that hurt too and I still remember it today! When Dad finally came to terms with the idea that he could no longer live alone in such a large house, he also decided to get rid of a lot of the heavy pieces of furniture he couldn't take with him or that he didn't need. His children weren't informed of any of this until we suddenly saw it had nearly all gone. We never knew what actually happened to the sewing machine until that day when Janet suggested I took a glance at the inside of 137 on that estate agent's web site I previously mentioned. Well, would you believe it? There it was, our sewing machine, after so many years, still sitting in the kitchen. Yes, it was definitely ours! What memories it brought back. All those ballet costumes and pretty party dresses Mum made for us. I remember, ah, those two pretty pink party dresses, exactly the same, one for me and one for Janet, with net underneath the skirt, to make it stand out when you swirled round, and a large bow at the back.

Another piece with a bit of a story attached is a very nice dark polished oval, wooden table with curved legs, on which we put the large wireless, then later the television, and then the gramophone and other ornaments. It had a certain status! Then one day it disappeared, following one of Dad's actions. Much later, I remember seeing this at my friend Norma's house and she still has it to this very day with an old wireless on it, so every time I go and visit her, I see this lovely table sitting in her lounge. We know it belonged to us. Of course, she insists it is hers!

The lovely, large round table in the kitchen, excellent for large family dinners, especially at Christmas, was a centrepiece to our family life. It was a very heavy piece of fine wooden furniture and difficult to move around, so quite often the conversation went back to getting rid of it, but we could never do it, as it was such a lovely piece of wood work. If this table could talk it would have such a lot of stories to tell, I am sure. I would have loved to have kept it but how could you fit in such a bulky piece? There is nothing like it today. However, sadly, when Dad moved out, it went too, probably to some antique furniture shop.

The nicest piece of furniture is sitting in my sister's house in Cupar, Scotland. It is an elegant writing desk with a drop-down leaf for writing- from the days when people used to write letters with pen and ink. Janet took this when Dad died and we had to move everything out of the house. I think she still has it. I kept the tallboy instead. It was part of my parents' bedroom suite and they used it to keep the bed linen and underwear in. It came with a large double wardrobe with a long mirror inside it and a double bed. A real bedroom suite which I suppose was quite modern for the times. After the war, furniture was quite basic but well made. The tallboy still has fond memories for me. It is now in my house in Italy and I use it to keep all my English teaching books well stored.

Another strange object I brought back to Italy when Dad died was what we called the 'bathroom chair'. It had been a very elegant 'Queen Anne'-style chair, but it had lost its padded seat, and had been repaired and banished to the bathroom to rest clothes on. It had been painted hundreds of colours over the years. When I wanted to re-furbish it, it took me days to get all the layers of colour off to find its original one. I still use it at home here in Italy to put my clothes on.

Another piece of furniture a new fixture in 137, which brings back painful memories, is the marble fireplace. It replaced the enormous black iron one. One day, when I was about four I think, it broke down and water flooded everywhere. I remember coming down in the morning to see Mum and Dad sweeping the water out of the back door. They were up to their ankles in it. Then, the new fireplace arrived and looked so modern. We had put a rocking chair next to it and of course I sat and rocked on it so many times I cut my forehead on the top corner not once but twice. It caused such panic as it bled really badly. but not to worry: just stick a thick ugly plaster on it and it will all go away. Well, it did not because when

Mum or Dad tried to take the plaster off, the deep cut just opened up again. I think I still have the scar on my forehead, and I think I still feel it.

Both Janet and I managed to salvage a few precious objects, just before Dad moved out of 137 without filling us in on the details. I managed to keep a few of my reading books, my first doll and other memorabilia such as my first Timex Cinderella watch, a dark red draw string purse and a Queen Elisabeth II crown money box, given to me in celebration of the Queen's coronation in 1952. Just a few small items that still mean a lot to me.

Chapter Six
Happy Days

137 was a happy house. I really remember it as being just that. When I mentioned in a previous chapter the 'entertainment room', I was referring to our back sitting room, which was the centre of all our fun, but in fact the whole house was full of fun, from the Christmas events in our sitting room, to the upstairs rooms where we played. We had so many friends and cousins to stay, birthday parties to celebrate, special Christmas dinners and so on, probably because it was such a big house and it was easy to invite people over to visit or stay.

My cousin John Mustin, from Birmingham, came several times and stayed for long periods as he was doing a course of some sort in Leeds. Cousins Pauline and Christine often came to stay at the weekend and we had great fun playing tents in my Mum's bed. We also had a few foreign exchange visitors who stayed for one or two months over various summers. There was Françoise from Paris, who came once on her own and a second time with her sister Onile. Then later Michelle and her sisters Pierrette and Danielle from the South of France, who came to stay on an exchange with Janet. My sister Janet studied French at Leeds Girls' High School and they organised exchange visits. She was very fortunate to spend some wonderful summers in the South of France. We really enjoyed having French guests stay with us. They were very friendly and we remained friends with them for many years. I also think we were very hospitable too.

The first time Françoise came we had quite a lively time. She was from Paris and quite a Parisian too. Looking back, she must have come from a well-off family as she had pullovers in every colour possible and she brought them all with her to Leeds. She wore a different pullover every day for the whole of the holiday, which did not go unnoticed. She also insisted on wanting to buy an original tailor-made kilt with an authentic tartan. Mum did her best to please her and meet her demands by going all over town searching for a suitable kilt, even though it would have cost the earth. Thankfully there wasn't enough time. Our French guest was impossible to please though. In England at the time we ate salad seasoned with salt and vinegar and that was it. No olive oil, like today. Françoise wanted olive oil on her salad which at the time did not exist in England, which was not yet in the Common Market (known today as European Union). The only olive oil to be found was at our local chemist, which was the sort used for medicinal purposes and so it came in a very tiny bottle. I am not sure how refined it was or if it was edible at all. I don't remember if Françoise enjoyed her salad more, but Mum did her best to please her and make her feel at home.

Another episode happened in 1964. My friend Lesley and I remember when we went to Fleetwood for a short Summer holiday and Françoise came with us. Unfortunately, she dropped her bikini out of her towel and lost it. She made us go to the Police station to report it missing and the local policeman asked her to describe it. How funny that was!

Both Janet and I always had birthday parties at home and Mum would prepare lots of lovely things to eat, from sandwiches and sausage rolls to the birthday cake itself. There was no buying ready-made food at 137! Both school mates and local friends were invited so there was always a large number of guests. We always played traditional party games which I have carefully handed down to my children Sarah and David, and I believe Sarah is now playing them with her children, Jamie and Dylan. Games such as "Pin the tail on the donkey", "Pass the parcel", "Hide and seek", "Musical chairs", "Musical statues", memory games and tasting games too. What fun we had. Only now can I appreciate how much hard work Mum put in so that we could have just three to four hours' fun.

I even had my twenty-first birthday party in our sitting room, my coming-of-age party. Dad bought lots of beer, a small barrel actually because now I could legally drink it! I invited lots

Image 10 - The Winteringham Family and Françoise in Fleetwood; photo taken by my friend Leslie (1964)

Image 11 - Dad holding bowls trophy in back garden (1968)

of people and it went on until after midnight, which was quite late in those days. We danced and had a good time. Bryan, Norma's brother, and his friend Bob came. He did his party piece of eating flowers I had been given as a present, which we thought was hilarious. "Charming!", as we would say then. He made everyone laugh so much. Music was provided by my record player so we had to keep stopping a lot to change the records. No music playing on loop like today!

When it was getting near Christmas, Mum would start baking. Half the fun was getting ready for the festive season. First, she covered the table carefully with a large tablecloth to protect it. She used to spread all the ingredients and equipment and start. She always made several Christmas cakes, mince pies, Yorkshire sherry trifles, scones, buns and so much more. Janet and I used to help her stir and mix. It was a big event. The kitchen and the living room were filled with the nicest fragrances. It all created an atmosphere of expectation, of waiting for the BIG day.

Although Christmases and our birthdays were never forgotten, we never really celebrated my Mum's or Dad's birthday. What a shame really! Janet and I were the lucky ones, I suppose.

137 was a happy house because we spent so many Sundays listening to popular wireless programmes, singing together, dressing up and putting on dance shows. If we weren't busy performing, we used to play board games. Later, when Janet and I were a bit older, Janet played

some pieces on the piano or we played some vinyl record singles, such as EPs or LPs, on my gramophone, which is now called a record player, and was given to me for my sixteenth birthday. One of my first presents as a teenager was a small transistor radio which I could carry around with me, which was a novelty compared to the enormous appliances we had in the living room. I used to like listening to Radio Luxembourg in my bedroom but it wasn't that easy to tune in and hear it well. Another radio station I really liked was Radio Monte Carlo but yet again it was often fuzzy. Then the pirate radio stations started up. They were basically stations on boats somewhere in the Irish Sea and totally illegal but they played all the latest 1960s sounds.

Of course, friends were always around to play and if it was too wet or cold to play outside we used to make up some fantastic games upstairs on the second floor.

We often had visitors too. Christmas was the occasion when the Winteringhams got together. We often went to my cousin Peter's house on Church Avenue in Meanwood but they also came to see us, usually on Boxing Day. There was Uncle Leonard and Auntie Mary and their son Peter. Then Auntie Rene and Uncle Fred with Pauline and Christine. Then Auntie Nellie and Uncle Earnest with Joan, Neville and Bryan. Their eldest daughter Eileen had already left England and had emigrated to Canada. Mum prepared a feast as usual and we spent the whole afternoon and evening in our sitting room playing charades or miming games and generally having a good time. It was a regular get together for many Christmases.

On Sunday mornings, when I was a bit older, Uncle Wilf came around with his Alsatian dog. He nearly always arrived at about ten o'clock in time for coffee, and then Wilf, Dad, Janet and I would go to Beckett's Park or Woodhouse Moor with our dogs. We often ended up at the pub, usually the Original Oak for a Sunday drink. Mum usually stayed at home getting lunch ready. She didn't seem interested in socialising. I think she preferred to stay home. During the year though we did sometimes go all together as a family. Mum only went to the pub alone with Dad a few times a year, maybe when the Bowling Season started in Spring, or when the pub held a small party, or at Christmas time, usually the 24th.

All my cousins except Jane used to come to our house regularly over Christmas. Uncle Cliff, Auntie Julie and Jane came up from Bromley, down South, once or twice to stay with us in Summer. One year, Jane came to stay with us on her own for a summer holiday too. We sometimes went on holiday all together to Clacton and also the Isle of Man.

Image 12 - Janet, her friend Linda Markham and Mum in back garden (1956)

Image 13 - Carol wearing chrinoline in back garden (1956)

Image 14 - Carol's 21st birthday with Janet and our dog Gyp in the Sitting room (1969)

Chapter Seven
Grandparents

By nature, we should all have four grandparents so when you are small it is difficult to understand why you haven't got four but only one or two. I was lucky anyway to meet two of my grandparents.

I never got to meet my Dad's Dad, Joseph Winteringham, who was a soldier, a military man as my Dad would say, and died in April 1932, aged 53. Nor did I meet my Mum's Dad, Albert Mustin, whom we know very little about even today.

However, I vaguely remember my Mum's Mum, my grandma Ruth Deeley. She lived in a very nice house at 48 Dowar Road in Birmingham. I remember going to see her on two occasions. I recall one visit in particular because it was the time someone spilt some tea over my ankle and foot and I got badly burnt. I recall sitting in her lovely garden with a lawn and flower beds. Although I didn't see her very often I used to write to her a lot. She would send me letters, and sometimes a present for my birthday. I think I learnt to write letters by writing to her.

I don't have any real memories of my Dad's Mum, Eliza, who died in 1952 aged 73. I do remember her staying at our house for several months when I was very small. She must have been quite old as she was an invalid and stayed in bed most of the time. Her bed was downstairs in the living room next to the door leading upstairs. I can vision it clearly even now but I don't remember ever talking to her or her talking to me. Mum took great care of her.

As children. we were never told very much about our grandparents' lives. Even as we grew older and perhaps more able to understand grown-up matters, we never got to know many details. Perhaps this was the way things were at that time: you just did not talk about family history. Unlike today, when we tend to trace back our ancestors and sometimes come across events we never expected which can no longer be explained. Since our two Winteringham family reunions in 2004 and 2015, lots of interesting pieces of information have come to light.

Chapter Eight
The Games we played

In my opinion, my generation, the Baby Boomers, was the last one to play on the streets. Streets then were much safer places than today and as children we spent hours and hours playing outside. When in 2015 I went to see the back of 137 Victoria Road as part of a Winteringham family reunion, known as the Norwoods, I was surprised to see the same telegraph pole standing just outside our gate. This pole was testimony to all our games. It was used time and time again when it was your turn to count for hide and seek, or to play "What time is it Mr Wolf?" and so on. We would play "Tig" running around the Norwoods with our large group of friends. I remember some names like Sholto, Susan Nutter, Andrea Rogers, one of the Roger girls, David and Ian Falgate, Robert Jackson, Lynda Markham and her brother Billy.

We used to play ball games, throwing the ball against the large high wall of David Falgate's house, opposite ours. There were all kinds of challenges, chants to learn and difficult tricks to study. Then the girls always played skipping games. We had several skipping ropes: one to skip on your own with and another longer one to skip with a friend or two, in a kind of match. We practiced forward-skipping, backward skipping, twisting the rope, then we also played with an even longer piece of rope when there were three or four of us. We had turns to jump in or out of the rope as it turned. We had to learn songs and chants too so you had to know what time to jump in or out. Quite a task but what fun. We played for hours like this, until it was dark, but never getting tired.

We were also very imaginative and created our own games. When Janet and I were very young, maybe five, we often took our prams with our dolls in them down to Burley Park for a walk. All of our friends came with us as it was a game of Mums and Dads. Burley Park was quite distant from our house, at least for five-year olds, plus the fact that we had to cross Cardigan Road, a busy main road with lots of traffic, although certainly not as much as today. We did it several times, coming back quite late when it was nearly dark. Our parents never told us off, although I imagine they must have been a bit worried. It was such an adventure.

Just up the slope of the Norwoods, turning right, you came to Brudenell Secondary School with its large playground. We used to go there to play on our bikes and roller skates as it was safe. I remember learning to roller skate there and also falling and hurting my shoulder, vouching I would never go skating again. In fact, it did put me off doing it again. I was very friendly with caretaker's daughter Margaret Nolan. Her Mum became very friendly with my Mum and she often used to pop in for a chat. We considered her a bit of a gossip but she was a good friend to my Mum, especially when she began to get ill. Unfortunately, the school was demolished some years ago.

When we were a bit older, I would say teenagers, maybe fourteen, my dear friend Norma and I would go around the Mayvilles on my bike looking for boys. Unfortunately, we only had one bike between us. My Uncle Cliff had given me one but Norma didn't have one so we had to share. That meant that one would cycle and the other would walk along side. We would ride around, up and down after school, and after tea in the early evening. Sometimes we met boys and talked. I had a crush on one good looking boy but I can't remember his name. Nothing came of it, though.

One early memory that comes to mind is when Dad used to take me to see his family on Jameson Street in Woodhouse, an area of Leeds, on Sunday mornings. I must have been about four. I took my first red tricycle and cycled all the way up to Woodhouse Moor, a lovely park at the top of Victoria Road. It had a large round, tarmacked area where children could skate or cycle. Woodhouse Moor was enormous and stretched on both sides of Otley Road. The far side had a fun fair every September. We would go firstly as a family and later on Janet and I would go on our own with friends.

Sunday afternoons were often spent at home especially in the colder months so of course we had to find things to do to occupy our time. Janet gave us a piano concert or we put the radio on and listened to "Sing something simple" and other singing programmes. We all joined in the singing together and learned the words off by heart. Some of the songs I remember are "Love and Marriage", "All I want for Christmas are my two front teeth" and "How much is that doggy in the window?", just to name a few. If we weren't singing we were dancing and putting on made-up shows. We spent so much time singing and dancing, thanks to the radio. No television entertainment back then! We also played lots of board games. Our favourites, that we played regularly, were Ludo, Snakes and Ladders, Monopoly, Draughts, as well as card games such as Snap, Beat Jack out of town, Old maid, Rummy or Whist, all played around our large table in the living room.

On those rainy days during our Summer holiday we often invited friends round to play and it was fun to play games in our house because it was so big. Of course, the most obvious one was hide and seek where we used to run all over the house, upstairs and downstairs, looking for someone. Then we had treasure hunts and "find the ring", all good excuses to run all over the house even more. What a noise we must have made but I do not remember ever being told off about it!

The most intriguing game we played, which was extremely imaginative in my opinion, was creating a spooky room in one of the upstairs bedrooms. We closed the curtains and turned the furniture around to make a scary trail with tents and other strange inventions. There were tunnels, climbing areas, under and over furniture. One friend at a time had to enter alone and go through this scary trail in pitch black. The rest of us waited outside listening to the screams and shouts of the adventurer. This was one of our favourite games and took quite a while to prepare. Half the fun was getting it ready.

On a more serious note, another activity I remember doing regularly every Friday with my Dad was counting money and putting the coins into stacks according to type. Dad for some reason had to count money and maybe he thought it would help me with my arithmetic and problem solving. It didn't!

As we grew older and with the coming of television, our entertainment changed a little. Of course, there were no programmes during the day and we had to wait for "Children's Hour" at five o'clock which lasted about an hour. I remember one of my favourites shows was "Lone Ranger", on his white horse and with his Indian friend Apache. It was a western. There were also cartoons I liked such as "Popeye" and "Tom and Jerry", although my Saturday teatime favourite was "Top Cat". On Saturdays we used to watch a detective TV series called "Dixon of Dock Green", followed by "Juke Box Jury", one of the first music programmes on BBC television. Later, when I was a teenager, I could not miss "Top of the Pops" every Thursday night. It was extremely popular with live bands playing songs from the hit parade. The programme saw many changes since the 1960s and, although it is no longer shown on TV, it lasted well into the Noughties. The first British Soap operas were also just starting up. One of the first was "Coronation Street" which we weren't allowed to watch. Dad did not consider it a good type of programme. Dad used to watch rugby matches on telly but he really loved a flutter on the horses so he often watched horse races which we were forced to bear.

Mum and Dad were members of a book club and used to buy books quite often through this system. In fact, one of our cupboards in the living room was crammed with old, well-read books.

Both Janet and I were both quite creative. We spent a lot of time making things, either painting or colouring. Dad would bring us lots of crayons and paints and other materials to use from work. I remember making several white plaster circus animals which we had to leave to dry out and then carefully paint. I also used to love doing jigsaws. All in all, we were quite imaginative and productive as most children were at the time.

Chapter Nine
The food we ate

As well as playing, singing and dancing, eating was also an important part of living at 137. I also think eating is worth a mention in my little book for two reasons: one because it gives an insight into what we ate just after the Second World War, when food was still scarce and rationed, and two to pay tribute to Mum who was a fantastic cook and took great pleasure in making some lovely family dishes.

As I said food was still scarce after the war and families were still on rations in 1948. I remember my Mum having a rations book so she could buy staple food like sugar, flour, milk and so on. She used to shop locally. There was a grocer's across the road which also included the Post Office. Next door was Nixon's, the newsagent's that also sold sweets and chocolate. There was a steep slope outside, down to the red Post Box and the red telephone box where everyone who had to make a phone call would stand in a queue for ages after 6 p.m. waiting for their turn. It was cheaper after 6 p.m. and not many people had landlines then. Most people used public phones so there were always long queues. Ours was very conveniently across the road so we could see when it was best to make a dash for the phone as the queue had dwindled down a lot.

The Post Box is still there today but the Phone Box has gone. Across the road, on the corner, was Jackson's butcher's. Mum bought most of her meat there, like stewing steak, liver, lamb or beef roast for Sunday lunch, and of course minced meat for our dog Gyp too. A short walk down on the same side of the road was the baker's and opposite there was a fruit and vegetable shop. You can see we had every kind of shop close at hand which made shopping very simple. There was also a Co-op down the road, a bit further away, where Mum used to go to do the big weekly shop because it had a stamp discount system. I remember Janet and I used to spend time sticking these stamps in a little booklet, usually on a Friday, until it was full and we could get a discount on certain foods.

Bottles of fresh milk and one of orange juice were delivered to our door early every morning and eggs came once a week from our local dairy which was the Co-op down the road.

Mum used to go into town (Leeds City Centre, that is, usually the market, to get some fresh fruit and vegetables for when she took students in because she needed larger quantities. It was cheaper but very heavy to carry home. I often went with Mum on a Saturday to help her carry all the heavy bags home. We used to walk from the market to the bus station and catch the number 56 bus home which dropped us off nearby.

I have already spoken a great deal about the kind of food we ate, but I feel I still need to say that our daily meals were always freshly cooked and very filling. Dad's breakfast was often bread and dripping or sometimes a bacon sandwich and a cup of tea when he had to go to work, but at the weekends we often had the typical English egg and bacon breakfast with a cup of tea. We did not always have a full breakfast, and we often just had a boiled egg or cereals. Cornflakes and Rice Crispies had just come on the market and were very popular but there was not the choice we have today. Later, as I grew up, I went off English breakfast and always had a slice of toast and marmalade with a cup of Nescafé instant coffee, which was quite trendy back then.

We always had a full Sunday roast and we often had Yorkshire pudding. I had dishes like fried egg and baked beans on toast for lunch, which was my favourite. Frozen foods did not exist when I was very little but when I was bit older I remember enjoying Bird's Eye fish fingers and mash. One of my favourite dinners was liver and onions, with peas and mash.

Sunday lunch was filling but we always had Sunday tea too. This was usually a lettuce and tomato salad with ham or pork pie followed by something sweet, such as a home-made cake and some tea.

Nearly every dinner time was followed by a pudding which could be a jam sponge and custard or a rhubarb crumble or a bread and butter pudding. On Sundays we nearly always had apple pie and custard but sometimes we had a variation. My favourite was bilberry and apple pie which left your mouth purple. And there was always a Jacob's cream cracker with butter and cheese to finish.

I really ought to mention the food Janet and I didn't like. Mum always cooked fresh vegetables to accompany the meat. If we had cabbage, brussels sprouts or cauliflower, there were terrible scenes around the table as we just couldn't swallow it and Dad would start shouting and telling us off. We had to clean our plates and the only way I managed to swallow brussels sprouts and cabbage was by adding a lot of vinegar.

Although everyone loved eating at our house, Janet was a real problem when she was little because she just didn't seem to like anything. Who knows why! She was so fussy and poor Mum had to come up with something she liked, usually bread and sugar or a banana sandwich. In order to keep the peace and quiet, I often ended up eating Janet's food because she refused to eat it and then Dad would start up again. At Christmas time, when Mum made some scrumptious dishes, Janet was quite happy to sit down to a jam sandwich. Little did she know what she was missing!

I remember when new foods appeared on the table, for example when bananas became available. They were really popular. Then when frozen foods became available Mum used to buy the occasional treat, maybe frozen peas, but she insisted on cooking fresh veggies and not buying the new convenience foods. One convenience food we often had was a cold dessert called "Angel's Delight", made by whisking milk into a coloured powder, usually strawberry or something very similar called 'blancmange'. Yogurt and many other convenience foods still didn't exist. We did not eat a lot of fresh fruit. The only fresh fruit were apples and pears when I was very young but   later there was a better choice such as strawberries, cherries and plums. Therefore, we often had tinned fruit like a fruit salad or tinned peaches, mandarins and apricots, served with carnation milk, the nearest thing you could get to cream. Carnation milk too came in a tin. We often had jellies on a Sunday in Summer. Mum made a trifle on special occasions, which is why it is still one of my favourite English desserts.

Chapter Ten
Keeping 137 in shape

137 was certainly a large house and so it was difficult to keep it up to date and fashionable. This was always one of the problems with 137 because there were always jobs waiting to be done. Some major tasks never got done either because they were too expensive or simply just too big to take on, like central heating for example. We often felt the cold in the winter months despite Mum's efforts to keep us all warm.

Our house, like most English houses, was fully carpeted. Each room had its own wall-to-wall fitted carpet which needed to be changed every so often. Then the staircases and landings were also all carpeted and there were three floors to cover. Even our bathroom was carpeted to make it feel warmer when you got out of the bath.

Every room was decorated which means they were wall-papered from floor to ceiling, each with their own particular colour and design. As a family we spent a great deal of time choosing the right colour matches and patterns for the room we had to do up. Janet's attic bedroom was blue and mine was pink with very similar flowery patterns. Of course. all this hard work was done in the family. It would be called DIY today. It was not common to call in a professional to do the job in those days. Everyone did their own decorating. I was tall and considered "strong" so I was often roped into helping out. At first, I did very menial tasks, rather like the errand girl, "Get this, get that!!", not forgetting also cleaning up afterwards, scraping off all the extra blobs of paint and so on. I did not mind doing it as it was rather an event and a change from routine. Later I got promoted to actual painting and even wall papering and in fact I became quite good at it. Being tall, meant I could help with fitting the wall paper at the top end. I thought it was quite a creative pastime and enjoyed it but I was not responsible for all the work and looking back it must have been very demanding and tiring for both Mum and Dad.

Chapter Eleven
Our dog Gyp

I couldn't possibly end my little story without giving a mention to Gyp as he was very much a part of our family and much loved. Gyp was a black and white mongrel. It is thought he was a mix between a whippet, rather like a greyhound race dog, and a terrier. He had a cute face with large expressive brown eyes and a white beard. He was a hairy dog but wiry and fast. I do not remember exactly how old I was when we got him but I must have been about seven or eight. Gyp was very tiny when we welcomed him into our home, maybe just a few months old, and he lived over thirteen years, which is a lot in 'dog years'.

Mum, Janet and I often used to walk home after Mrs Reed's dancing lessons, down Queenwood Drive, past the school, past the Hyde Park Picture House, and on toward home. It took about 25 to 30 minutes. One summer evening, on our way down the hill, we heard a sort of whimpering but we couldn't make out where it came from. This happened a few times and each time we talked about it, trying to understand where the noise was coming from. Finally, one evening we decided to investigate. We walked down into one of the side roads until we came to a back yard, and in the corner, we saw a tiny black

Image 15 - Our new puppy Gyp

Image 16 - Our dog Gyp

bundle all curled up in the corner whimpering. We tried to catch his attention but at first he was very wary and wouldn't come close. We did not give up. Then he came up to us, his little tail wagging so fast, and it made us decide there and then to take him home. And we did. I suppose it was stealing in a way but he was definitely ill-treated and not well looked after. We thought we were doing the right thing, saving him from a life of misery.

We did not really know if we were going to keep the little dog. Maybe just for a few days, Mum said. Of course, we all took to him and decided we could not let him go. We called him Gyp, and to this day I still have no idea why. The idea was that we all looked after him but as it is with these things Mum was usually the one who did all the work. She was the one who took him on his morning walks, bought his daily share of mince, fed him twice a day and then took him on his evening walk every day for I don't know how many years. When Janet and I got older, we often took Gyp for a walk too. The joy on his face when we said "Get your lead!". He would cock his head on one side, wait, then jump up and down in excitement. He would run up and down the stairs until he was mad. All this for a walk! He seemed to understand everything we said to him.

Our favourite walk was to Burley Park, which was quite nearby and there was plenty of space for Gyp to run. We walked over the bridge, and

Image 17 - Gyp enjoying snow in the back garden (1964)

*Image 18 - Janet taking Gyp for a walk in Burley Park
(1966)*

before we even got into the Park, he was pulling with all his might. We could barely keep up with him. His favourite pastime was running beside a passing train. He raced and chased it. He loved it and ran so fast he even kept up with the train until it disappeared out of view. On Sundays it was Dad's turn to take Gyp on a long walk, and not just a short 'round the block' walk. He often met up with Uncle Wilf who had an Alsatian and together they went off to Beckett's Park, a little bit further away but in the vicinity of the Oak pub, Dad's favourite Sunday lunchtime haunt. Sometimes Janet and her friend Linda went too. It became a family outing.

Once we went on holiday, I don't remember where, maybe Fleetwood, where pets weren't allowed so we were forced to leave him in kennels for a week. We did not want to leave him but we hoped for the best. Gyp must have been home sick and missed us a lot judging by all the welcome licks and kisses we got when we went to pick him up. He would not stop jumping for joy. He was a very happy dog just like 137. At Christmas he was treated like a child or as one of the family. He was given suitable "doggy" presents, such as rubber bones to chew, a new lead or a toy. When I came to Italy, Gyp even sent me a Christmas card!

Gyp lived with us all his life. When Mum died, and Janet and I had moved away, and Dad was living alone but still working, Gyp became difficult to look after. He was alone all day with no-one to take him out and no company. As he got older, he began to lose his eyesight and he often bumped into things and hurt himself. Dad one day took the decision to have him put down. It must have been heart-breaking. I still do not know to this day how he had the courage to do such a thing. However, it was for the best. Dad took him for his last walk to Burley Park not far from the RSPCA and then came home alone. We still talk about Gyp even today for he is still in our thoughts.

Chapter Twelve
The Last Chapter

My Dad continued to live at 137 even after Mum died in June1972. Both Janet and I had moved away for study and work reasons, although we still returned home during holiday periods. Dad was still working for E.J. Arnold's, a well-known Leeds company that provided school and educational supplies to schools in Britain but also abroad. It must have been very hard to keep 137 in order when you are out at work all day, mainly because it was such a big house. Obviously, Dad no longer used a lot of the rooms and he was also beginning to have problems with his legs. It was then decided it would be better for him to find a bungalow or a one-storey flat. He had a long wait but he eventually moved out of 137 about 1980. Neither Janet nor myself were there when he moved out, which was a shame in a way for several reasons. One was that we never really said goodbye to the house I had lived in for over 24 years, which was a bit sad. It was the house I left when I got married in September 1974. Secondly, because we never got the chance to choose what we wanted to keep or take with us. Dad was quite ruthless and threw a lot of our stuff away. We also had so much big heavy furniture that, although it was good lasting quality, it just didn't fit into modern houses and was cumbersome to move anyway. We later discovered Dad had given away a lot of this furniture and sold other pieces, but only later did we find this out!

I suppose we forgot about 137 for a while as we were busy with our new married lives and small children. It was not until much later, maybe after Dad died in February 2000, that an interest in our old house came back to us. First, we just went for a drive down Victoria Road, past 137, then on another occasion we walked down it and actually stopped to get a better look at it. Since then we have been back several times taking our grown-up children and grandchildren to see it.137 is still standing and looking well, despite its age. It certainly must have been a much loved house. Of course, my only regret is that 137 is no longer a family home but it has been changed into flats or bedsits for students. Our lovely blue Front Door is still there and kept its colour. Its porch with its beautiful old worn out tiles still has its original doorbell although I do not think it works but underneath there are lines of four or five small modern doorbells that do not do justice to a once splendid house like 137!

On our last visit to Leeds for a Winteringham family reunion in 2015, Janet's family and my own walked from Headingley down Bainbrigge Road, past my first Primary School on Spring Bank Lane, down Cardigan Road and up Victoria Road to have a look at 137 and the back of the house. The old telegraph pole we used when we played our street games, like "What time is it Mr

Wolf!", was still there. Each time we go back, the house brings back so many happy childhood memories that I simply had to put them down on paper for others to enjoy. I hope it has made happy reading for all!

Image 19 - Carol and Janet outside 137 Victoria Road in 2015

www.ingramcontent.com/pod-product-compliance
Lightning Source LLC
Chambersburg PA
CBHW061038050726
47592CB00004B/1503